Animal
STORYBOOKS

P9-CRT-135

The Kangaroos' Great Escape

Story by Rebecca Johnson
Photos by Steve Parish

GARETH STEVENS
GS
PUBLISHING
A Member of the WRC Media Family of Companies

Please visit our web site at: www.garethstevens.com
For a free color catalog describing Gareth Stevens Publishing's list of high-quality books
and multimedia programs, call 1-800-542-2595 (USA) or 1-800-387-3178 (Canada).
Gareth Stevens Publishing's fax: (414) 332-3567.

Library of Congress Cataloging-in-Publication Data

Johnson, Rebecca, 1966–
    [Kangaroos' lucky escape]
    The kangaroos' great escape / story by Rebecca Johnson; photos by Steve Parish. — North American ed.
        p. cm. — (Animal storybooks)
    Summary: As a group of kangaroos, exhausted from trying to escape a fire, meets a dead end, a wallaby comes to the rescue.
    ISBN 0-8368-5971-5 (lib. bdg.)
    1. Kangaroos—Juvenile fiction. [1. Kangaroos—Fiction. 2. Wallabies—Fiction.] I. Parish, Steve, ill. II. Title.
PZ10.3.J683Ka   2005
[E]—dc22
                                               2005042874

First published as *Kangaroos' Lucky Escape* in 2002 by Steve Parish Publishing Pty Ltd, Australia.
Text copyright © 2002 by Rebecca Johnson. Photos copyright © 2002 by Steve Parish Publishing.
Series concept by Steve Parish Publishing.

This U.S. edition first published in 2006 by
Gareth Stevens Publishing
A Member of the WRC Media Family of Companies
330 West Olive Street, Suite 100
Milwaukee, Wisconsin 53212 USA

Gareth Stevens series editor: Dorothy L. Gibbs
Gareth Stevens cover and title page design: Dave Kowalski

Printed in the United States of America

1 2 3 4 5 6 7 8 9 09 08 07 06 05

A big red kangaroo
was the first
to notice danger.

4

With a thump
of his strong back feet,
he was off.

The gray kangaroos sensed danger, too.
They smelled smoke!

They bustled
their joeys
into their pouches
and bounded away.

Parents called
to their sons,
"Stop fighting!"
It was time
to move on.

As the wind grew stronger, the blazing fire grew bigger and more fierce.

The kangaroos hopped away from the fire at full speed.

12

A rock wallaby stood
on a large boulder, watching
the kangaroos from a distance.
He had seen the fire, too.
The wallaby knew
that the kangaroos'
only escape
was to reach
these rocky cliffs.

He watched as some kangaroos became exhausted and stopped to rest. Many of them would be too tired to climb the rocks even if they reached them.

With the help
of another wallaby,
the rock wallaby
came up with a plan.
He took off, rapidly
heading toward
the top of a cliff.

When the little wallaby
reached the highest point, he
stopped and looked around.
Then, just as quickly as
he had gone up the rocks,
he bounded back down.

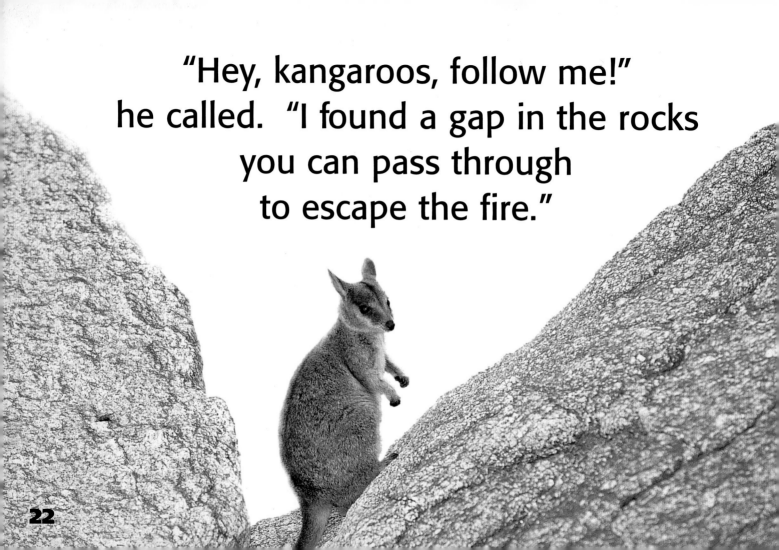

"Hey, kangaroos, follow me!"
he called. "I found a gap in the rocks
you can pass through
to escape the fire."

The kangaroos
followed the wallaby
through the rocks
to a place where
they could rest
and take a long,
cool drink of water.

At last, they were safe.